GEOGRAPHY *for fun*

Ecosystems

Pam Robson

Copper Beech Books
Brookfield, Connecticut

Produced by
Aladdin Books Ltd
28 Percy Street
London W1P OLD

First published in the United States
in 2001 by
Copper Beech Books,
an imprint of
The Millbrook Press
2 Old New Milford Road
Brookfield, Connecticut 06804

Editor: Kathy Gemmell

Designer: Simon Morse

Illustrator: Tony Kenyon

Picture researcher: Brian Hunter Smart

The author, Pam Robson, is an experienced teacher.
She has written and advised on many books for children
on geography and science subjects.

Printed in UAE

Cataloging-in-Publication data is on file
at the Library of Congress.

ISBN 0–7613–2422–4

CONTENTS

INTRODUCTION

Geography is about people and places and all the changes that take place in the world. What ecosystems are and how they are breaking down. How the climate affects wildlife in different parts of the world. How human progress is forcing wildlife to adapt to change. How the homes of birds and other animals are being destroyed. Geography is about all these things. You need to know about ecosystems so that you can help wildlife survive and flourish.

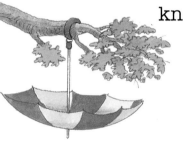

1 Watch for numbers like this. Each step for the projects and surveys inside the book has been numbered this way. Make sure you follow the steps in the right order to make the projects and complete the surveys.

FEATURE BOXES
● Watch for the feature boxes on each double page. They either give extra information about the project on the page, or they suggest other interesting things for you to make or do.

WHAT'S HAPPENING

● The What's Happening paragraphs explain the geography behind the projects and surveys.

● Watch for Helpful Hints on some pages—they give you tips for doing the projects.

● Look in the Glossary at the back of the book to find out what important words mean.

● Always use an up-to-date atlas to find where places are.

WARNING

● This sign means that you must be careful. Ask an adult first if you want to conduct a survey of a woodland, pond, or seashore. Always check the times of tides if you walk along a seashore. Never go out alone. Always tell an adult where you are going and what you are doing.

WHAT IS AN ECOSYSTEM?

The natural home of a plant or animal is called its habitat. Each habitat supports a different community (group) of living things. An ecosystem is made up of any given habitat and its community. The living things in an ecosystem interact with each other. They also interact with the nonliving parts of their environment (surroundings), such as water or weather. Ecosystems can be large or small. A pond or even a tree is a small ecosystem. Our planet is one huge ecosystem. The study of ecosystems is called ecology.

LOCAL ECOSYSTEMS

Make a local ecosystems map.
If you can, choose an area with buildings and open spaces. You will need a large-scale map of the area, colored pencils, and a notebook.

Lichen on stones

Ants on wall

Bird's nest

Frog's eggs

1 Use the large-scale map to sketch or trace an outline map of your chosen area. Draw in the roads and buildings. Ask an adult to walk around the area with you.

2 Make notes or take photos of different ecosystems. There are often small ecosystems within larger ones. Look for living things interacting with nonliving things, such as insects on a wall.

3 Mark on the map the locations of all the ecosystems you have observed, using different patterns or symbols for each ecosystem. Draw the symbols with pencil first, then color them in.

4 Each ecosystem should be easy to recognize. A meadow, for example, could be shown by a tuft of grass. Design a key to explain the symbols and patterns you have used. Print names beside each one.

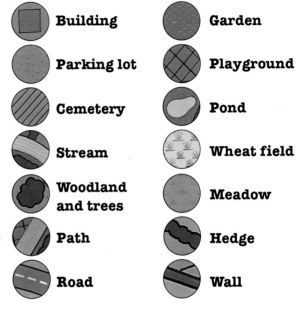

- Building
- Parking lot
- Cemetery
- Stream
- Woodland and trees
- Path
- Road
- Garden
- Playground
- Pond
- Wheat field
- Meadow
- Hedge
- Wall

Litter

5 Now add to your map any other details you have observed. Depending upon the season, you may have noticed a bird's nest or a fox's lair. Or you may have noticed parts of an ecosystem damaged by litter pollution.

LIVING AND NONLIVING

● An ecosystem is a jigsaw puzzle of living and nonliving parts. The Sun and weather play a part in every ecosystem. Each part is vital. They are interdependent—if one piece is lost, the whole ecosystem breaks down. Make a list of the living and nonliving parts of your ecosystems.

Ecosystem	Living parts	Nonliving parts
Pond	Frogs, dragonflies, water lilies, pondweed	Water, stones, air, sunshine

WHO EATS WHAT?

All living things in an ecosystem depend upon each other for food. They are linked together in a food web. In a healthy ecosystem, there must be a balance between the number of living things that exist there. This balance is called the food pyramid. Usually, there are far fewer carnivores (meat eaters) than herbivores (plant eaters). The carnivores keep the number of herbivores under control. Most natural ecosystems, on land and in water, get their energy from the Sun. The Sun's energy is passed through the food pyramid.

FOOD PYRAMID

4. Large carnivores eat herbivores and small carnivores. So they are both secondary and tertiary (third-level) consumers.

3. Small carnivores eat herbivores. They are secondary (second-level) consumers.

2. Herbivores are primary (first-level) consumers. They eat green plants directly. They are prey to large and small carnivores.

1. Plants are producers—they produce their own food using energy from the Sun.

FOOD WEB

Food webs show all the members of an ecosystem community and how they interact with each other. Make your own food web to show who eats what.

Person

Bird of prey

Rabbit

Sheep

Plants

Air

Sun's energy

1 Cut out pictures of living things found in a wood. Draw and cut out a picture of the Sun, water, and a cloud (for air). Glue your pictures onto folded strips of cardboard.

2 Stand the cards up. Use ribbon and tape to attach each animal to its food. Use red ribbon for carnivores and green ribbon for herbivores. Trace each ribbon with your finger to see how all the plants and animals are interlinked.

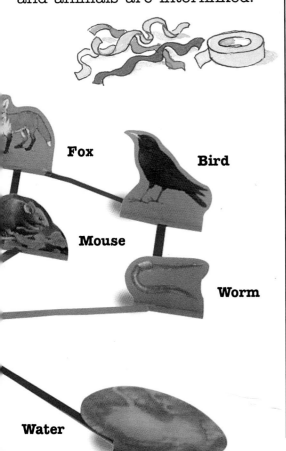

Fox

Bird

Mouse

Worm

Water

ENERGY FROM THE SUN

● Each chain of links in a food web, joining plants to herbivores and carnivores, is called a food chain. Most food chains start with the Sun.

● Chlorophyll, the green color in leaves, uses the Sun's energy to make food. Sunlight turns molecules of water and a gas called carbon dioxide into sugar inside the leaf. This process is called photosynthesis.

Sugar

● In this simple food chain, a cabbage makes food using sunshine. The Sun's energy passes to the caterpillar when it eats a cabbage leaf. A bird then eats the caterpillar. When the bird dies, decomposers —small creatures and plants such as insect larvae and fungi—break down its body into the soil. This enriches the soil, which plants then use to help them grow.

Sun

Cabbage

Caterpillar

Bird

Larvae and fungi

AN OAK TREE

An oak tree supports a small ecosystem. The tree is broad-leaved and deciduous, which means it loses its leaves in winter. The oak is a rich habitat for animals and birds, which find food and building materials on and around the tree. At ground level, there are worms, insects, leaf litter, dead wood, flowers, grasses, and fungi. From the ground beneath the tree to the canopy—the top of the tree—a variety of living things can be observed.

WHAT'S IN A TREE?

Make a seasonal diary for the ecosystem of an oak tree. You will need paper, string, twigs, an old umbrella, and colored pencils.

1. Hang the open umbrella from a lower branch on the tree. Shake the branch lightly. Describe or sketch any minibeasts that fall into your umbrella trap. Record your findings, then return the minibeasts to their habitat.

Spring

Date/time	Weather	
April 12th 11 A.M.	☀️☁️	
April 15th 1 P.M.		**Squirrel**—gray
April 16th 4 P.M.	🌧️	**Worm castings**—lots on ground under tree
April 18th 10 A.M.	☀️☁️	**Green woodpecker**—green body, red on head, making a drumming noise on tree trunk
	☀️	**Primrose**—pale yellow flowers, 5 petals, short stems, thick, dark leaves
		Wood ants—running up tree trunk

2 Ask an adult to help you press some twigs firmly into the ground around the tree. Use string to make a circle on the ground around the twigs. Write down, sketch, or photograph anything you see inside the circle, such as worm castings, old acorn shells, and leaves.

3 Look for small mammals and birds, such as crows, magpies, or even a sparrow hawk, in the tree. Are any birds nesting? If there is a hole in the trunk, there may be a woodpecker's nest. Listen for bird songs.

Wood louse—gray; body like armor

Jay—blue, black, and white feathers

Titmouse—

4 Write headings, for time, date, and weather. Write in your observations and stick in sketches, photographs, and even bark rubbings. Add labels to build up a complete picture of an oak tree ecosystem.

ON AND UNDER OAKS

● As seasons change, the oak tree menu changes for the wildlife in and around it. In the fall, large birds and mammals eat acorns. In spring, jays and magpies eat eggs stolen from nests. Titmice eat caterpillars on leaves and buds.

● Nature recycles its waste. Under a tree, you will find decomposers that feed and grow on dead plants and animals, breaking them down into the soil (see below). Decomposed matter does not hold energy, but provides the soil with nutrients (goodness).

Fungi grow on dead logs and leaves.

Ants, beetles, and other small creatures eat droppings and fungi.

Bacteria break down anything that remains.

GLOBAL ECOSYSTEMS

The world is split into large ecosystems called biomes. Biomes are named after the main type of vegetation (plant life) that grows there. They are shaped by climate—how hot, cold, wet, or dry a place is. Tropical forests have lots of rain and sunshine. Deserts are hot and dry. The tundra (cold desert) is freezing. Mountaintops are also cold. Temperate areas have a warm, moist climate and are rarely very hot or very cold. Each place has its own food web, with wildlife that has adapted to the climate there.

Tundra
Coniferous forest
Temperate grasslands
Temperate forest
Mountains
Desert
Scrub
Savanna
Seasonal tropical forest
Tropical rainforest

Climate depends upon latitude (how far north or south of the Equator a place is), and altitude (height above sea level).

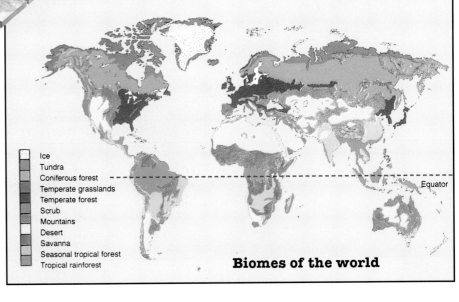

Ice
Tundra
Coniferous forest
Temperate grasslands
Temperate forest
Scrub
Mountains
Desert
Savanna
Seasonal tropical forest
Tropical rainforest

Equator

Biomes of the world

ISLANDS
● Islands often have unique ecosystems. The Galapagos Islands, off the coast of Ecuador, are home to some of the world's rarest creatures, such as giant tortoises and sea lizards (right).

BIOME CARD GAME

To make this game, you will need thin cardboard, scissors, and colored pencils. Each set of cards shows a food chain in a different biome.

1 Cut out 30 pieces of cardboard. Copy the pictures on the cards shown here, until you have two sets of each food chain and six Sun cards. Number and label each set, as shown.

Temperate forest set

x 2

Sun (all sets)

x 6

Tropical rainforest set

x 2

Tundra set

x 2

Desert set

x 2

2 Two or more can play. The aim is to collect four cards belonging to the same set. All sets must include a Sun card (1). Each player begins with four cards. Take turns to pick a card from the pile. Either keep that card or replace it at the bottom of the pile. The first person to collect a whole food chain is the winner.

ADDING MORE CARDS
● Find out about more food chains, in these or other biomes, and make cards for them. Make sure you always have a plant, a herbivore, and a carnivore. Make up a symbol for each new biome.

CONIFEROUS FORESTS

Coniferous trees have soft wood and needlelike leaves that stay green throughout the year. They grow best in cold climates and on mountainsides. In a coniferous forest, sunshine rarely reaches the forest floor, so ecosystems are not nearly as rich as in broad-leaved forests, because few plants grow with so little light. The diversity (variety) of wildlife is not as great, because there are fewer plants for animals and birds to eat. There are not many natural coniferous forests left today—most are now planted by foresters.

Dry

Crossbills use their special beak to extract seeds from inside pine cones.

Most conifers are pines, firs, or spruces.

Few plants grow on the dark forest floor.

Chipmunks hibernate in winter.

Canadian coniferous forest
1. Crossbill
2. Douglas fir
3. Canada geese
4. Owl
5. Spruce
6. Lynx
7. Moose
8. Chipmunk
9. Weevil

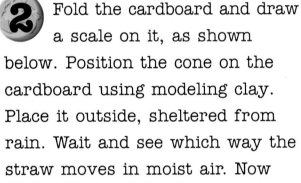

Wet

CONE GAUGE

Use a pine cone to make a hygrometer. This measures humidity—moisture in the air. You will need a pine cone, a pushpin, a plastic drinking straw, cardboard, modeling clay, and a pen.

1 Stick the pushpin into one of the middle scales of the cone. Push a straw over the end of the pushpin.

2 Fold the cardboard and draw a scale on it, as shown below. Position the cone on the cardboard using modeling clay. Place it outside, sheltered from rain. Wait and see which way the straw moves in moist air. Now label the scale "wet" at one end and "dry" at the other end.

WHAT'S HAPPENING

● Pine cones hold the seeds of conifers. They close when the air is moist and it is about to rain, to protect the seeds inside. The outside scales absorb the moisture in the air, swell up, and bend inward to close.

Seed

SUSTAINABLE FORESTRY

● In many parts of the world, the wildlife-rich natural vegetation has been cut down and replaced by coniferous forests. The conifers are then cut down to make paper and furniture. Now foresters practice sustainable forestry. This means they cut down only part of the coniferous forests at one time so that ecosystems can survive.

TROPICAL RAINFORESTS

Many of the world's plant and animal species live in tropical rainforests, where the climate is always warm and moist. The Amazon rainforest in South America is like a huge row of apartments, with different species living at each level. At the bottom is the dark forest floor, then the herb layer, shrub layer, understory, canopy, and, at the top, the emergent layer. Hardwood trees grow tall and straight as they struggle to reach the sunlight. They are so tall that they have roots above the ground.

Emergent layer—the tallest trees push through the canopy to reach the Sun.

Understory—younger trees strive to reach the sunlight.

Herb layer—ferns and herbs grow. Tapirs and insects live here.

Canopy—treetops are bound together by creepers and climbing plants. Home to orchids, birds, monkeys, snakes, and lizards.

Shrub layer—young trees grow from seedlings. Woody plants with large leaves and colorful flowers grow here.

Forest floor—rotting leaf litter covers the poor soil. Few plants grow here, except along rivers, where some sunshine gets through.

MINIRAINFOREST

To create a minirainforest, you will need a small fish tank with a lid (or use plastic wrap), soil, charcoal, gravel, and suitable plants, such as ferns, mosses, orchids, and African violets.

1 Line the bottom of the tank with a layer of charcoal and gravel. Cover with a layer of soil. Make the soil damp before arranging your plants.

2 Arrange the plants before planting. Do not put them too close together as they will need room to grow.

3 Place the lid (or plastic wrap) over the tank and put in a warm spot, but not in direct sunlight. Water every few weeks. The lid will keep the soil moist.

WHAT'S HAPPENING

● Rainforests play a big part in controlling the world's climate. Without trees, there would be less rainfall. Leaves transpire, which means they lose water through tiny holes. Transpiration helps make the air moist. The leaves on the plants in your tank will transpire and keep the air and soil moist.

● Thunderstorms are frequent in rainforests as the warm, moist air rises quickly and cools.

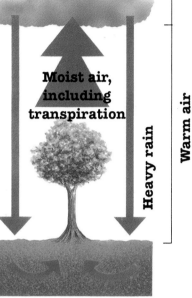

Fast-rising moist air condenses into droplets, which form high thunderclouds.

Cool air

Warm air

Moist air, including transpiration

Heavy rain

Soil is kept moist

EPIPHYTES

● Epiphytes are rainforest plants that grow on other plants. Some grow in the low, darker parts of the forest. Others, like orchids, like the sunshine of the canopy.

DEFORESTATION

● Half the world's rainforests have been destroyed. Some people cut down trees to farm the land for food. Others cut down trees to sell the lumber.

HOT DESERTS

Living things struggle to survive in hot, dry deserts. Many have learned some very strange habits, just to stay alive. The spadefoot toad, found in the Sonoran Desert of Arizona, hibernates underground for most of the year. When the annual midsummer rain approaches, it emerges to mate and lay its eggs in pools of rainwater. Within days, the eggs hatch and become tadpoles, then toads. Then the toads disappear underground again. Desert plants have to survive for long periods

without rain. Many survive as seeds. Cacti have shallow roots, close to the surface, ready to catch any rain that falls.

PLANT A DESERT GARDEN

To create a desert garden, you will need a shallow clay bowl, sand and soil, pebbles or gravel, protective gloves, and some small cactus plants. Ask at your local plant nursery for advice on which cacti to buy.

 1 Mix together the sand and soil. Fill the bowl three-quarters full with the soil mixture.

2 Put on protective gloves, then plant your cacti. After planting, cover the surface of the soil with pebbles or gravel.

Gila monster

DESERT ANIMALS AND PEOPLES

● Desert animals have had to adapt to hot, dry conditions. In North America, a poisonous lizard called the Gila monster stores fat in its thick tail. It can live on this fat for months without eating. Birds called roadrunners save energy by running instead of flying. Ground squirrels in the Kalahari Desert in southern Africa use their plumed tails as sunshades.

● For thousands of years, the only people living in the Great Australian Desert were Aboriginal nomads—people who regularly move from place to place. Now, most Australian Aborigines live in towns and cities. Bedouins have lived in the deserts of North Africa and Syria for centuries. A few still live as nomads, traveling from oasis to oasis.

Bedouins

HELPFUL HINTS

● Place your desert garden in a sunny position.
● Cacti have sharp spikes, so handle them with care. Use thick leather or suede gloves to protect your hands when handling cacti.
● Do not water your garden too often. Cacti need only a small amount of water. Too much water will cause the stems to rot and will leave a black mark.

COLD DESERTS

Cold deserts, called tundra, are places where the ground is frozen for much of the year. Alpine tundra is found at high altitudes, above the tree line. In the Arctic, there are no trees, only grasses, mosses, and lichens. Lichens are fungi that contain algae. They appear as crusty patches or shrubby growths on rocks. Shrubby lichens can only survive in clean air. They are an important part of tundra ecosystems, and are threatened by pollution, which can be carried a great distance by winds and water.

North of the tundra is the Arctic icecap.

Below the surface is permafrost, which is ground that is frozen all year round.

The tundra has rocky mounds, called pingoes, and long lakes.

Below the tundra is a belt of coniferous forest, called the taiga.

LOOKING FOR LICHENS

One way to check pollution in your area is to look for lichens. The nature and color of any lichens will indicate air quality. If you find only green algae, the air is probably heavily polluted.

1 Ask an adult to come with you to look at local lichens. Look on walls, stones, trees, and gravestones. Record the color and location of any lichens you see. Sketch their appearance. Check the scale opposite to help you identify the lichens.

2 Mark your lichen findings on the ecosystems map you made on page 6. Make up a key to show the type of lichen found. Write down the date on which you found them.

on page 6

Polluted

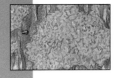

GREEN ALGAE
Found in heavily polluted areas. Probably no lichens.

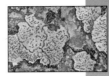
GRAY-GREEN CRUSTY LICHENS
Often found on gravestones. High-level air pollution.

ORANGE CRUSTY LICHENS
Also found on gravestones. Medium-level air pollution.

LEAFY LICHENS
Found on walls and trees. Low-level air pollution.

SHRUBBY LICHENS
Found on rocks and trees. Clean air.

Clean

Lichens can live for 4,000 years. They can survive all climatic conditions. There are 25,000 known species. They grow slowly, only half an inch a year.

SYMBIOSIS AND CAMOUFLAGE

● Symbiosis is a partnership between two living things, from which both benefit. The fungi and algae that make up lichens are symbiotic. The fungi absorb water and minerals, then the algae use these to turn

sunshine into food by photosynthesis (see page 9). Both the fungi and algae gain from living together.

● Camouflage is the ability of certain animals to blend in with their natural surroundings and so hide from predators. But predators also use camouflage to hide from their prey.

see page 9

Arctic fox in summer

Arctic fox in winter

FRESHWATER ECOSYSTEMS

In ponds and lakes, where the water is still, plant life is rich. Rivers and streams have running water, so there is less plant life. Large predators like perch eat smaller fish. Too many predators in a pond destroy the ecosystem because the secondary consumers are all eaten up. Without secondary consumers to control numbers, the primary consumers increase and eat all the plant life. Without plant life, the pond ecosystem breaks down completely.

ZONE 3: DEEP WATER

ZONE 2: SHALLOW WATER OR SWAMP

Great reedmace

Arrowhead

Water lily

Water crowfoot

Milfoil

POND ZONES

Pond animals move around, but plants remain in one place. Make a pond chart, dividing it into zones according to the plants found there. Be careful near water. Always tell an adult what you are doing.

1 Make sketches and take notes about the plants in and around the pond. Look first at the bank, then at the shallow water, or swampy area around the edge, then at the deep water. Here, you will only be able to see the tops of the plants. Some plants live completely under the water.

Meadow sweet

Marsh marigold

Great pond sedge

Water iris

2 Sketch a cross section of the pond and divide it into zones, as shown here. Zone 1 is the bankside, Zone 2 is the shallow water or swamp area, and Zone 3 is the deep water. Underwater plants, called submerged aquatics, go in the deep water zone. Fill in details about each plant. Use a field guide to help you identify any plants not shown here.

POND LIFE

● Birds that live and feed near fresh water have adapted special feet and beaks. The heron has a long, thin beak with which to catch fish or frogs. It has long legs so it can stand for a long time in deep water waiting for prey.

Flamingo

Avocet

Heron

● Everything in a pond food web depends on plant life, even if you cannot see any plants. Big fish eat small fish, which eat dragonfly larvae, which eat tiny creatures, which feed on microscopic plants.

Dragonfly

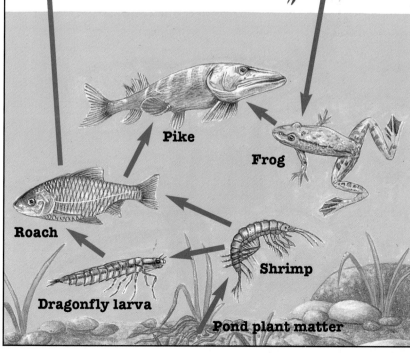

Pike

Frog

Roach

Shrimp

Dragonfly larva

Pond plant matter

ON THE SEASHORE

There are sandy, pebble, and rocky beaches. Each provides a different habitat, but all are affected by the same tidal movements. There are two high and two low tides every day. Very high tides, called spring tides, happen twice a month. Between high-water spring tide marks and low-water spring tide marks, there are five seashore zones. In these zones, plants and animals have adapted to produce a variety of ecosystems. Different seaweeds and shells are found in each zone.

BEACHCOMBER

Next time you go to a beach, carry out a beach ecosystem survey. Tell an adult where you are going and ask a friend to come with you. Always check the times of high tides. Carry out your study at low tide. Select a quiet stretch of beach to study.

Splash zone

Upper shore

High tide mark

Middle shore

Lower shore

1 Stretch a length of string from the top of the beach to the edge of the water. Hold each end in place with a pebble. Mark the string with a pen where you think each zone ends. The five zones are lower shore, middle shore, upper shore, high tide mark, and splash zone.

2 List the differences you notice between the zones. Collect shells, pebbles, and small pieces of seaweed and driftwood. Note carefully which zone you found them in. Record the date, time, and weather conditions.

JETSAM

● Storms at sea often carry jetsam (trash from ships) onto beaches. Ropes, bottles, and cans are found among seaweed and shells after bad weather. Containers holding dangerous chemicals have been found on beaches. They can gradually alter ecosystems.

SAND DUNES

● Grasses have long roots that hold the sand down in ridges. This prevents the sand from blowing away. Grasses are often planted in sand dunes to stop the sand from blowing any farther.

ROCK POOLS

● Rock pools are left behind when the tide goes out. Plants and animals that live in rock pools cannot survive out of water. In rock pools you may find sea anemones, crabs, sea urchins, starfish, seaweeds, and shrimp. Small fish are also found in pools. Always replace rocks that you move.

3 Map the area of beach you have surveyed onto a sheet of cardboard. Draw in the zones created by high- and low-water marks. Glue on and label everything you have collected.

Rock pool

SALTWATER ECOSYSTEMS

The ocean is the largest habitat on Earth. But sea animals depend upon plants for their food, just as land animals do. The most important marine plants, called phytoplankton, are so small that they can only be seen with a microscope. Phytoplankton are the primary producers in the food chains of the sea. They grow near the surface, where sunlight causes photosynthesis to happen. Microscopic animals called zooplankton then feed on phytoplankton, and larger animals eat the zooplankton.

Orca

Tern

Seal

Squid

Fish

Krill

OCEAN FOOD WEB

Phytoplankton are single-celled algae. If you get a chance, look at a sample of sea water under a microscope, and you will see the pretty patterns on phytoplankton.

Zooplankton

Phytoplankton

SALTY FACTS

Blue whale

● A food web of the sea includes some of the smallest and largest living things in the world—the blue whale and krill. Krill are tiny shrimplike forms of zooplankton, found in the seas of the Antarctic. Amazingly, they are the only food the blue whale eats. The blue whale can be over 90 feet long. It strains the krill from the ocean through the baleen inside its mouth, which acts like a strainer.

Krill

1. Corals grow around a volcanic island.

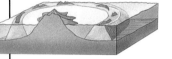

2. The volcano erodes and a lagoon forms.

3. The volcano sinks completely. The reef remains with small, sandy islands on top.

● In tropical seas, there are low islands called coral reefs that are formed by tiny creatures called polyps. The jellylike polyps build up hard skeletons of calcium carbonate. When they die, the skeletons are left as coral. New polyps grow on top of the dead ones. Coral needs warmth and light, so it grows only near the ocean's surface.

● Coastal mangrove swamp forests are types of tropical forest. Mangrove trees have adapted to survive in the salty water in mud estuaries of tropical rivers. They have special roots that keep the leaves above the water and allow the plant to obtain more oxygen. Mangroves are the habitat of many species, such as fiddler crabs, and are breeding grounds for reef fish.

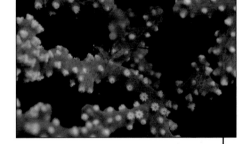

WILDLIFE GARDEN

As your contribution toward preserving healthy ecosystems, you could make a wildlife garden. Even if you do not have your own garden, you can encourage wildlife by cultivating plants in a windowbox or on a balcony. Plant flowers with strong colors and scents that will attract insects such as bees and butterflies. Peacock butterflies like to lay their eggs beneath nettle leaves. These pages will give you some ideas on how to create a wildlife garden.

A SPACE FOR WILDLIFE

Diversity is the key to a successful wildlife garden. Diversity means providing many different habitats—shady areas, sunny spots, and open spaces. This will attract many creatures. You could make a habitat pile, from logs, to attract insects. Make a bird table so birds can feed safely. You could even build a pond.

HELPFUL HINTS

● Choose the east- or west-facing side of a tree trunk for a birdhouse. A south-facing nest may harm fledglings because they will become too warm.

● A log pile will encourage minibeasts into your wildlife garden. It will also encourage small birds like wrens which feed on insects.

● Leave an area of garden with long grass—this will also encourage minibeasts.

BIRD FEEDER

Make environmentally friendly pine cone bird feeders. You need some long pine cones, a ball of string, a spoon, unsweetened peanut butter, birdseed, waxed paper, and a baking tray.

1 First, cut a length of string for each pine cone. Loop and tie the string to one end of each cone.

2 Use a spoon to smear peanut butter all over each pine cone. Make sure it covers every part of the cone. Press firmly into all the spaces.

3 Sprinkle birdseed onto the waxed paper on the baking tray. Roll the cones in the birdseed until they are all well covered. The birdseed will stick to the peanut butter. Shake off any loose seed.

4 Birds like to feed where they are safe from predators like cats. Position your pine cone bird feeders away from shrubbery, trees, and fences. A tree stump or bird table in the center of an open space is a safe site.

CONTRACT WITH NATURE

● As houses and roads are built, animals and plants are losing their natural habitats. Even common birds like sparrows are disappearing. Remind yourself to do what you can to encourage wildlife by making a contract with nature.

Contract with nature

I ....

Promise ....

....

....

....

....

Signed ....

ECOSYSTEMS IN DANGER

The habitats and the wildlife that together make up ecosystems are in danger. Tropical rainforests are especially rich in animal and plant life. It is thought that they contain between 60% and 80% of all the land species on Earth. Some species there are now threatened with extinction.

Rainforest destruction

● An area of rainforest the size of 37 football fields is lost every minute, to provide wood or farmland.

● The tiny golden lion tamarin of Brazil's Atlantic coastal rainforest is threatened by the loss of its habitat. Today, there are only about 700 left.

About 90% of Brazil's Atlantic coastal rainforest has now been destroyed.

S. America

Golden lion tamarin

● A parrot called the Spix's macaw also lives in the Brazilian rainforest. Although there are a few captive birds, there is now thought to be only a single wild one left.

● One fifth of the world's tropical forests are found in Africa. In the Congo Basin, ten million acres of forest are destroyed each year to clear the ground for farming. In 1999, five central African countries signed the Yaounde Declaration, an agreement to save huge areas of forest in the Congo Basin.

Amazing survivors

● The Australian thorny devil can survive in its desert environment without drinking. It gets moisture from the black ants on which it feeds. Grooves on its skin channel moisture from dew into the corners of its mouth.

● The eggs of the fairy shrimp can survive for 10,000 years until water activates them.

● The hawkmoth caterpillar has a clever disguise—the patterns of its body make it look just like a snake!

● A chameleon catches its fast-moving insect prey with its tongue, which can move much faster than its body.

GLOSSARY

bacteria (sing. **bacterium**)
Single-celled organisms (living things) found in soil that help break down dead matter.

biome
A large ecosystem, usually named after the type of vegetation that grows there.

camouflage
The use of color or pattern that enables an animal or plant to merge with its surroundings.

carnivore
A meat eater.

climate
The average weather in a place over the year.

community
The plants and animals within one habitat.

consumer
An animal or plant that eats other living things.

decomposer
An organism that breaks down dead plant and animal matter, releasing minerals into the soil.

ecology
The study of ecosystems.

ecosystem
One community in one habitat and its nonliving environment.

environment
The surroundings of a habitat.

epiphyte
A plant that grows on another plant without feeding from it.

habitat
The natural home of a plant or animal.

herbivore
A plant eater.

hibernation
Long sleep taken by some animals to save energy when food is scarce.

lichen
An organism composed of two living things, algae and fungi.

photosynthesis
The process that plants use to make food, using sunlight and chlorophyll (the green color in plants).

phytoplankton
Microscopic plant life found on the surface of oceans.

predator
An animal that hunts and eats other animals.

prey
An animal hunted and eaten by a predator.

producer
A green plant that makes food through photosynthesis.

symbiosis
A partnership that benefits two different species.

vegetation
Plant life, especially of a particular region.

zooplankton
Microscopic marine animal life that feeds on phytoplankton.

INDEX

PICTURE CREDITS
Abbreviations: t-top, m-middle, b-bottom, r-right, l-left, c-center.
All photographs supplied by Select Pictures except for 5tl, 10ml, 17br—
Digital Stock. 15bl—Rolf Bender/FLPA-Images of Nature. 18ml—Jurgen
& Christine Sohns/FLPA-Images of Nature. 20c—G T Andrewartha/FLPA
-Images of Nature. 22ml—Ian Rose/FLPA-Images of Nature. 25tr—David
Hosking/FLPA-Images of Nature. 26ml—Corbis. 27mr—Stockbyte.